DEDICATION:

For my real life magically brilliant boy, Zachary. You inspire me every day and have changed me for the better.

For all children who are differently unique and perfectly imperfect, you are ALL magic.

ACKNOWLEDGEMENTS:

A HUGE thank you to my husband, JR, and my amazing boys, Corey and Zachary. My life would not make sense without you. Also to my family and friends, thank you for always keeping me centered and grounded in this crazy, wonderful life of mine.

ISBN 978-0-9990959-0-4

magicallybrilliant@gmail.com

The Magically Brilliant Boy

by
Kristy Gray

An adventurous journey into the fascinating life of a young boy with Autism.

Original Art by
Deborah Burow

There is a teeny tiny world

of a Magically Brilliant Boy

that turns out
to be

oh so BIG

Movies, like magic, play over and over in his head.

WARD STOP

PLAY BACK

The story of the life he lives.

BACK and FORTH
FORWARD and REWIND

HAPPY Birthday

5

He is smart as a fox and learns quick on his feet, he'll always keep you guessing.

His brilliance is remarkably sweet.

7

He CIRCLES and climbs and CIRCLES some more.

Around and around he goes.

Flying like a leaf in the BREEZE.

8

He is funniER than the funniest,
funny one you know.
Happiness is the aiR that he breathes.

MAGiC
show
Today

11

LOOK!

12

He swims like a fish
born to the sea.

The ocean is his magical
getaway.

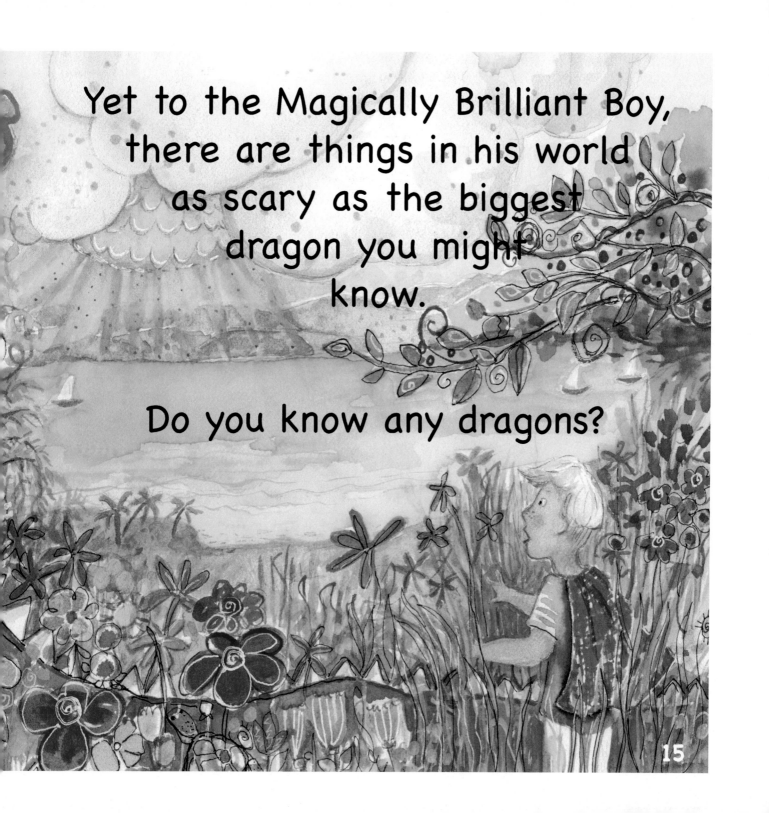

Yet to the Magically Brilliant Boy,
there are things in his world
as scary as the biggest
dragon you might
know.

Do you know any dragons?

Dragons can be

objects or people or sounds. . .

. . .things that make him afraid.

Too many

PEOPLE, faces, and

sounds . . . SiReNS of all kinds,

ringing phones and moRE,

scaRE the Magically Brilliant Boy

right down to his toES.

A restaurant, a mall, an amusement park or zoo, can be overwhelming and make his brain feel sad.

POPCOR

20

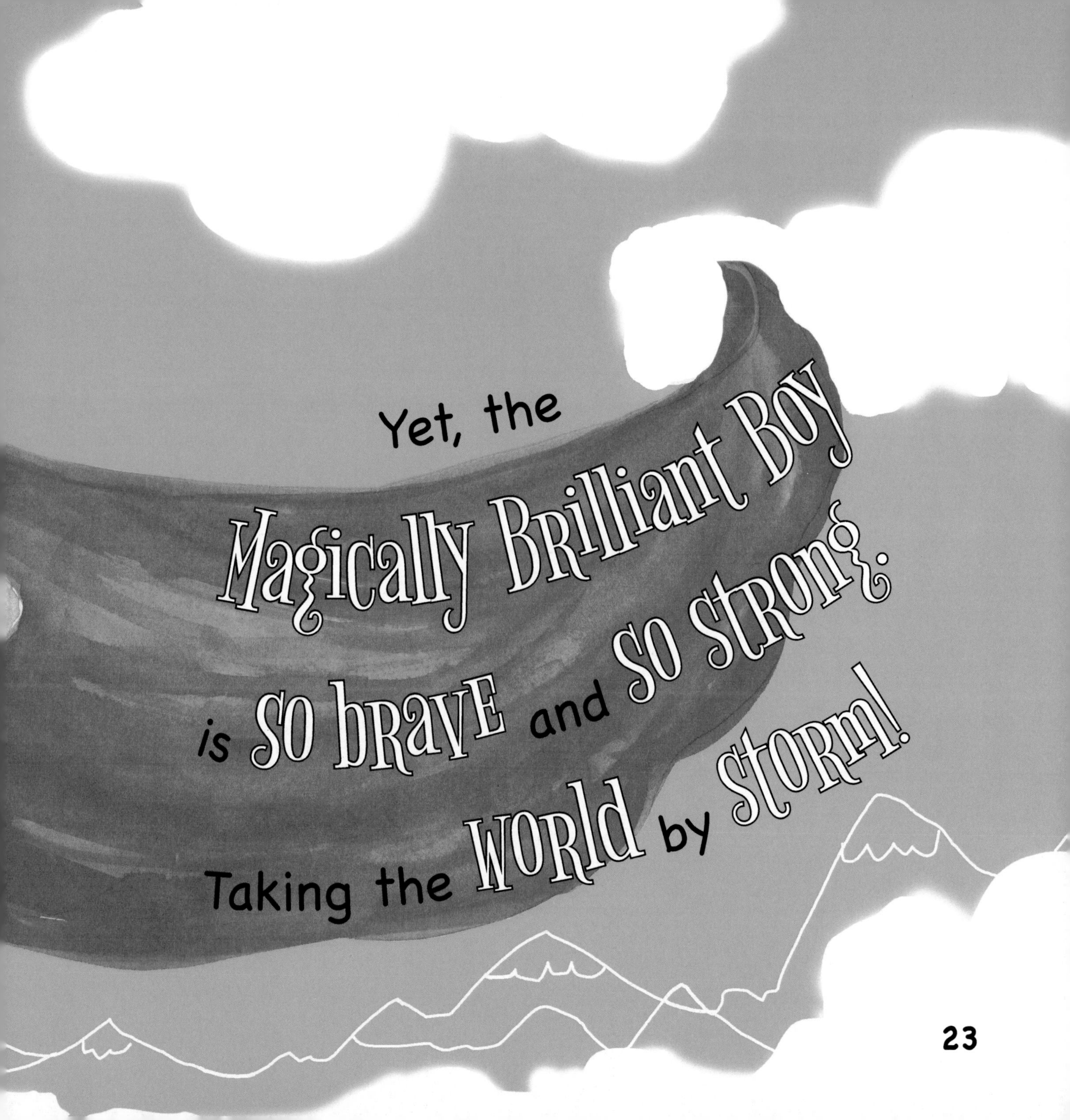

Yet, the

Magically Brilliant Boy

is SO BRAVE and SO STRONG;

Taking the WORLD by STORM!

The Magically Brilliant Boy has dreams to move mountains,

just not all the words to set those dreams free.

He doesn't *quite* seem to need many WORDS, to say SOMETHING OH SO BIG.

To the Magically Brilliant Boy, the world is grand and vast, confining and small.

28

His world is
both scary
and safe.

The **Magically Brilliant Boy**,

holds all of the answers quietly
inside . . . as we all keep asking the questions.

How does the rain make you feel?

Who is in your family?   do you know that I love you?

Are you happy?

Do you understand me?

Can you sing the weather song today?

what are you feeling?   what are you thinking?

How can I help you?

Can I play with you?

Can you tell me your phone number?

why do you like to spin?

Why do you get so upset?

Do you need the bathroom?

This **Magically Brilliant Boy**

is **safe** and **sound,** surrounded

by all that he **needs.**

There is **happiness** in each

smile he **breathes.**

33

Just like the world around him, he is differently **unique, perfectly imperfect,** the very same as **you** and **me.**

34

The greatest gift of the

Magically Brilliant Boy

is his . . .

... OH SO BIG magical love!!

"The moon makes the **tidE** go **in** and **out** . . ."

38

. . . but LOVE makes the WORLD go 'ROUND."

— Zachary G.

39

Kristy Gray

A high-energy, devoted and loving mother of two boys, Kristy and her husband of 24 years, JR, raised their family in Northern New Jersey, where they both grew up and still reside. As a lover of life, family, and core values, Kristy works hard to maintain a humble existence while pushing herself forward to fulfilling all her dreams.

Photo by: Dana Catapano

As a mom raising a child with Autism, Kristy has opened up her world to you and invited you into her daily life with her son through "The Magically Brilliant Boy." She does not claim to be an expert, simply a mom with a lifetime of experience.

Kristy's reason for writing "The Magically Brilliant Boy" was to give readers a glimpse into the inner workings of her son's existence. She hopes the book will open the world of autistic children to everyone and hopefully to create a deeper understanding.

Deborah Burow

Deborah is an artist who fills her illustrations with tiny, vibrant, imaginative details. She delights in creating hidden treasures, sprinkling them throughout her artwork.

She loves to see children and adults smiling as they look around and wander through her illustrations. So much to see. Happy art.

Photo credit: Suzanne Szalay

Living at the seashore influences her art in every way. Sailboats bobbing, starfish twinkling, deep blue seas rolling, puffy clouds dancing along the horizon, all add to the whimsy of her creations. All Deborah's artwork is a result of the joy that lives inside her. To see more of her work, visit www.deborahburowart.com.

magicallybrilliant@gmail.com